COLOUR GUIDE

EXTERIORS

MAIN CHAPEL

PORTICO OF GLORY

CHAPELS OF THE APSE CHOIR

CHAPELS OF THE LEFT NAVE

MUSEUMS

TRANSEPT

EX LIBRIS

DAVID JOHN BREEZE

QUICK VISIT GUIDE

CATHEDRAL
IN
SANTIAGO DE COMPOSTELA

Jesús Precedo Lafuente

© ALDEASA ®: 1993

Legal Deposit: VI. 195-1993

I.S.B.N.: 84-8003-006-2

Design and Layout: Juan M. Domínguez y Rosa Mayer

Editorial management: Ana Cela

Translation: SAT/CB

Photographs: Manuel González Vicente, Incafo* y Oronoz**

Photomechanical Production: Gama Color, S.A.

Printed in Spain by: Heraclio Fournier, S.A.

Cover illustration: Engraving by David Roberts (1796-1864)

TABLE OF CONTENTS

Partial view of the Obradoiro Façade.*

PREAMBLE

THE FOUR PLAZAS

Four plazas surround the cathedral in Santiago. Two of them bear the names of age-old trades : Azabacheros Plaza, to the north, previously named after the old Romanesque façade and renamed in the 19th century in tribute to the jewelers who worked withthe black mineral, jet; and Paraíso Plaza, meaning paradise dedicated to the Virgin Mary and built in homage of the mystery of the Immaculate Conception, as defined by Pope Pius IX in reference to the

dogma of Christian faith. To the south is the Plaza de los Plateros, dedicated to silversmiths. To the west is the plaza dedicated to stonecutting — Cantería; it is the work of several generations of craftsmen, who laboured with hammer and chisel to interpret the mysterious language of stone. And finally, to the east, "La Quintana do los Muertos", the Plaza of the Dead, once a cemetery but today perfectly worked in stone and stretching from the cathedral to the Benedictine Monastery of San Pio de Anteamares.

General View of Santiago de Compostela.*

Azabachería Square.

Platerías Square.

Quintana Square.

Obradoiro Square.**

THE THIRD CATHEDRAL

The cathedral is Romanesque in style, its construction having been begun in the year 1075. However, over the centuries it has incorporated elements from later artistic periods, which points to the degree of accomodation embraced by its rectors vis-à-vis the ever-changing tastes of each epoch. Some of these later elements are completely new, in the sense that they have simply been added on to original Romanesque features. Others have actually altered the original features, as in the case of the Azabachería and Obradoiro façades.

This is actually Santiago's third cathedral. The first was built in the times of Bishop Diego Peláez, the second during the reign of Alphonse VI. There still remain perfectly identifiable vestiges of these two earlier cathedrals, both of which were closely linked to Kings Alphonse II and Alphonse III. The remains of these churches — which were in no way comparable to the current cathedral — are situated close together near a necropolis and what remains of the old city walls and defensive structures, just below the cathedral. It should be noted that the cemetery, which served the town for practically the first 8 centuries of the Christian Era, has been instrumental in confirming the existence of the early, poorly documented settlement that has become modern-day Santiago de Compostela.

Cathedral miniatures. Register A. 12th and 13th centuries.

The Tomb of the Apostle.

THE NAME "COMPOSTELA"

The name of this cathedral town is Santiago de Compostela, though that hasn't always been the case. At first it must have been a site of sacred reverence, due to the discovery of the remains of St. James the Apostle (Santiago in Spanish). It also must have been called Arca Marmórica (Ark of Marble) at one time. It wasn't until later that the Apostle's name was added to Compostela. Many readers will have heard that the word Compostela comes from "Campo de la Estrella", or Field of the Star. However, while this is an ingenious and not totally unfeasible etymological supposition, there are indications that the real root of the name denoted a well-kept tract of land or sepulchre, which, if nothing else, is certainly no less Jacobean an explanation than the other.

The "Field of the Star" folk etymology, still widely embraced by many Compostelans, most probably comes from the celestial light show that guided the hermit Pelayo, in the 9th century, to the site where he claimed to witness a divine phenomenon, which he later described to King Alphonse II and Bishop Teodomiro. The Prelate, whose see was located in Iria Flavia just 17 kilometers from Compostela, was so moved by the hermit's account that he chose to be buried at the sacred site. In fact, his tomb can be seen today, inside the cathedral.

EXTERIORS

I THE OBRADOIRO FAÇADE

We could start our tour at any point in or around the cathedral, so for practical reasons we shall begin with the exterior. The Obradoiro façade was built in the 17th century to replace its Romanesque forebear, the features of which were completely discar-

General View of Obradoiro Façade.**

ded and, thus, lost on what today is known as the Portico of Glory. It faces west; and somewhere between the compassion for the damage incurred by its polichromed features through the relentless passage of time and the exquisite taste of Baroque exhuberance was born the great opus of Master Fernando de Casas y Nóvoa. He worked with many artists, among them the sculptors and woodcarvers Gregorio Fernández, Antonio Vaamonde, Lens, Gambino, Nogueria, Pose, López, Ramos y Montero and the painter García Bouzas. To the lower parts of the original Romanesque towers were added the Baroque towers of La Carraca, to the north, and Las Campanas (the bells) to the south, the latter of which is, in large part, the work of Master Peña de Toro. Regard-ing the figures on the Portico, St. James is seen with two disciples, Anastasio and

Image of St. James, Obradoiro Façade.

Theodore. Next to this motif are St. James the Lesser, St. Barbara, St. John the Evangelist and St. Susan.

Two stairways, both from the 12th century, lead from the square up to the cathedral itself. Beneath the stairways is a church inaccurately known as the Old Cathedral. It was built in the effort to avoid more costly storage facilities for building materials transported from afar. Three other buildings close off the square. The one directly behind us is a palace named after the Archbishop Rajoy, who had it built as a consistory and residency for the cathedral's priests. Currently it houses the City Government and the offi-

General view of former Royal Hospice, currently Ferdinand and Isabella Hostal.

ces of the President of the Galician Regional Government, or Xunta. To the right is the College of St. Hieronymus of Artists, from the 17th-century, though it incorporates the 15th-century doorway from the building that occupied the site previously. To the left is the Royal Hospice, founded by Ferdinand and Isabella for the pilgrims and today, a hotel.

II PLATERIAS

The Platerías façade is the only one that has preserved its Romanesque structure, albeit with modifications and added figures originally from other placements around the cathedral, which makes a sound interpretation of it somewhat difficult. However, it appears that the main motif is Christ, the Light of the World, with a mythological background scene possibly reinterpreted by the Christians. The main motif consists of Christ the King surrounded by saintly figures. At Jesus' feet is Abraham, looking up in admiration at his celestial descendant. The figure below this might be Moses, given the horn-like protuberances that are clearly visible and which were often used to depict the emanations of light said to shine from the patriarch's face following his encounter with Yaweh. There are also five apostles, though due to damage only three are identifiable: St. John, St. Peter and St. James. Within St. James' halo, there appears the identif-

David, Platerías Façade.

Partial View of Cathedral
from Platerías Stairs.*

Platerías façade. The creation
of Adam.

Platerías Façade Wall.

ying Latin inscription, Iacobus Zebedei. St. James is framed by two tree trunks, possible cypresses. To his right is the monarch who had the cathedral built, also identified by an inscription: "Alfonso Rey" (Alphonse the King). Worthy of special note is the statue of David playing the viola, on the left side of the entranceway. On the left tympanum are the temptations of Christ. The right tympanum is divided into two parts: the upper represents the Adoration of the Magi, while the lower contains scenes from the Passion. The original work of this façade has two signatures, those of the Masters Bernardo and Roberto.

Column Detail, Platerías Façade.

III THE CLOCK TOWER

The Plateresque construction on our left is the work of Rodrigo Gil Hontañón, from the 16th century. The echeloned tower at the southern extreme is called the Treasury because it.houses ornaments and other valuable church objects. The tiers, almost Asian in appearance, appear to have been influenced by native structures in the Americas. Certain writers content that these towers were designed as an homage to the Divine Mother. There is another, closer to the Fonseca building, which is known by the name of Torre de la Vela.

To the right is the **Clock Tower**, a blend of Gothic and Baroque elements. The first part is a kind of Gothic cube that the Archbishop, Rodrigo del Padrón, had built in the 16th century. It was given the name Berenguela, perhaps because Archbishop Berenguel de Landoira had it reinforced for better defence against the attacks of the Compostelan bourgeoisie, though some believe that it was actually named after Queen Berenguela, who cut a particularly slender figure. The Baroque portion of the tower was the work of Domingo Antonio de Andrade, a 17th-century craftsman. The current clockwork itself was built in El Ferrol by Antelo in the 19th century. The faces have only hour hands, while the two recently restored bells chime on the quarter-hour and the hour, respectively.

Treasury Tower.

Clock Tower.

Detail, Clock Tower.

The Door of the Saint, General View.

IV QUINTANA AND PUERTA SANTA

The cathedral's eastern square is known as Quintana, another word for plaza. The upper part is called Vivos (the living), and the lower, more ample part, de Muertos (of the Dead). This was the cemetery for many, many years. The huge wall face directly across the plaza from the cathedral forms part of the Benedictine Convent of St. Paio de Antealtares, once a monastery that was closely related to the St. James religious sect and a refuge where the Benedictine monks alternated with the St. James prebendaries. The cathedral had its great apse completed with nine others, either circular or many-sided in shape. And, over time, new buildings were constructed, some for the religious sect, others for defence and still others for offices that would tend to undo the initial architectonic harmony. It was precisely for this reason, in fact, that the cathedral's chapter decided in the 17th century to remodel the site, a project that was undertaken by Vega y Verdugo and put into practice by José de la Peña. Of the doors on this side, the most striking is the one called The Royal Door, the farthest to our left.

The Door of the Saint is opened on 31 December of each year designated as "Jubilar", meaning celebratory, in honor of St. James. Once inside, we see a smaller, Romanesque door, one of

The Apostles and Prophets on the Door of the Saint.*

Figures on Door of the Saint.

the nine the cathedral had. The exterior façade was done in the 17th century. The 24 small statues adorning it, representing apostles and prophets, come from the stone choir sculpted by Master Mateo. The three larger ones topping the façade are the work of Pedro Docampo; sculpted in the year 1694 they represent the Pilgrim Apostle and his two disciples Anastasio and Theodore.

V THE AZABACHERIA FAÇADE

We are now going up the Quintana stairway and leaving behind us the Corticela Parochial Church on our left, a structure with an Oratory that possibly dates from the 9th century. The St. Paio monks used to go there, even after the Monastery of St. Martín Pinario was built. It currently serves a widely secular function, as it is a a parish church for foreign visitors.

The Azabachería façade takes its name from the mineral crafts-

View of Azabachería Façade from Stairs.

Detail, Azabachería Façade.

men (who worked in jet), to which the street that gives onto this north-side square was once dedicated. The old name for this façade, according to the Calixtine Codex, was Paraíso, or Paradise, which was derived from the tales expressed in its Romanesque sculptures. This was where the so-called French Route of the pilgrimage came to its long-awaited end. Here, in this façade, we can see the first signs of Compostelan neoclassicism. Some of the artists who worked on it were Ventura Rodríguez, Lucas Ferro Caaveiro and Clemente Fernández Sarela. The latter two actually started the façade but discrepancies arose and the project was awarded to Domingo Lois Monteagudo, a student of Ventura Rodríguez who probably did nothing more than modify the iconography. Gambino sculpted the statue Faith. Máximo Salazar did those of St. James the Pilgrim, the kings Alphonse III and Ordoño II, and the portraits of Charles III and Marie Amalia of Saxony,his wife.

CATHEDRAL'S INTERIOR

❙ MAIN CHAPEL

We can enter the cathedral through this door. The first thing we see will be the main altar, which was constructed directly over the Apostle's tomb. The work carried out in the Baroque Period, under the direction of the Prebendary Vega y Verdugo, erased all the Romanesque elements, which had already been modified to a certain degree in the 15th and 16th centuries. The ciborium, or canopy, had to be adapted to the available space — which is why it is asymmetrical, though doubtlessly of great beauty. It was done by Domingo Antonio de Andrade. Other artists who worked on the main altar were: Francisco de Antas and Bernardo Cabrera, as Masters; the marble engravers were the Flemish artists Gutier, Sameria and Broces; the sculptures were principally the work of Pedro del Valle and Mateo de Prado, while the woodcarving was carried out by various Compostelan artists.

There are three images of St. James forming part of the main altar. Vertically, starting from below, we can see St. James the Master, from the workshop of Mateo; then we have St. James the Pilgrim and St. James the Knight, the latter of which was done by Mateo de Prado. Honoring St. James are four Spanish kings who played special roles within the Jacobean sect: Alphonse II, Ramiro I, Ferdinand V and Philip IV. The four corners are decorated with representations of the four cardinal virtues: Prudence, Justice, Strength and Moderation. The choir's woodcarving, completed once the former choir had been removed from the centre of the cathedral, was designed by Martínez Pidal y Pons Sorolla and carried out by Del Río in 1949. Regarding the lamps, we should mention

General View, Main Altar.*

Main altar's pulpit.

Image of the Apostle, Main Altar.

Pulpit details of scenes of the life
of the Apostle.

three: the one to our right, donated by María I; the one to the left, from Archbishop Monroy; and the one in the centre, from the Prebendary Diego Juan de Ulloa.

The main altar was rebuilt by Constenla in 1879. The silver was donated by the Archbishop, Fray Antonio Monroy, who shipped it from his country, Mexico. With the silver sent by the prelate, who was born in Querétaro, Antonio de Montaos fashioned the frontispiece and locutory; Juan de Figueroa did the sacrarium and the exigete, while the image of the Virgin Mary, designed by Manuel de Prado, was rendered by Francisco Pecul.

The two pulpits are the work of the Aragonese artist, Juan Bautista Celma. The one on the left has scenes from the tabernacle that were done by Antonio de Arfe. The one on the right also has episodes relating to St. James the Apostle, all of which are based upon the idea of the Saint's special protection of Spain.

II APOSTLE'S NICHE

Decorative Details, Pulpits.

The pilgrim comes to give his embrace to the stone image of St. James, seated like a master. It is polychromed stone, from the school of Master Mateo. The Archbishop Monroy donated the shoulder cape and the staff, which were worked by Figeroa. The origin of the embrace of the Apostle undoubtedly has to do with the great joy experienced by the pilgrim, who having completed his obligations, among them confessing his sins, then goes like the prodigal son to reconcile himself with the father-in-faith of all Spaniards. It is said that before the halo had been added to the statue, the pilgrims would place their hats on the Apostle's head so as to facilitate the embrace. Over the pilgrim's head is the votive lamp, made from the silver of the weapons of the Grand Captain, who donated it in 1512 when he went to Compostela as a pilgrim himself.

St. James' sepulchre, with the Saviour and the Apostles.

III SEPULCHRAL CRYPT

After leaving the statue's niche, one should visit the tomb of St. James and his two disciples, Anastasio and Theodore. The visitor may wonder how St. James the Apostle came to rest in this remote part of the world, in Finisterre. The legend has it that St. James came here to spread the gospel. If this is true, and the testimonies to this effect date from before the discovery of the crypt which occurred after a period of scant enlightenment in the 9th century, it is not difficult to accept that the Apostle was indeed buried in Compostela. The crypt is at the head of a burial ground dating from the 1st to the 4th centuries, looking towards Quintana de Muertos. Apart from that period of relative abandon, ended in the 9th century in the times of Bishop Teodomiro and King Alphonse II, the apostolic remains were against hidden during the incursion of the Englishman Drake in the 16th century and were not rediscovered until 29 January, 1879. The successive remodeling carried out over the centuries makes it impossible to know exactly how the actual site looked in antiquity. There are sufficient vestiges, however, to give us a general idea. It was certainly a Roman construction, dating from the 1st and 2nd centuries and similar to those found at other sites. It had two chambers: a lower one, the sepulchre itself, and an upper one that served as the oratory and a place for mourners. From an historical perspective, it is important to keep in mind the

Detail, Sepulchre of St. James.

evolution of the successive structures that were built, the Moorish invasion and the many remodeling efforts that affected the site, especially in the 12th and 14th centuries.

The work on the current crypt was begun in 1879 in keeping with the orientations provided by the historian and prebendary, López Ferreiro. An attempt was made to adorn the crypt in such a way that the new decor would evoke the old. In July of 1884, the silver urn was put in place; it holds in three compartments the three bodies, which had been reconstructed and catalogued by leading professors at the Compostelan medical school. The crypt occupies the original burial site, though on a higher level, since the current crypt actually corresponds to the upper chamber of the original Roman structure. The urn, designed by Losada, was fashioned by the Compostelan silversmiths Rey and Martínez. It is an imitation of the altarpiece, which was situated behind the altar and dates from the times of Archbishop Gelmírez, who lived in the 12th century. On the cover is the labarum, or ecclesiastical banner, with the monogram of the Greek name for Christ, an X and a P, the equivalents of J. and R; on the front and sides, the Saviour, framed by ovals or almonds; and, beneath the arches, the Apostles. On the altar is a crystal cross, a gift from Archbishop Gaspar de Zúñiga y Avellaneda in 1569.

Rear View of the Portico of Glory.

Towards the Portico

The visitor should now walk through the middle of the centre aisle to the Portico of Glory, which was, together with the western-most part of the cathedral that was lost when the Obradoiro façade was built, a doorway leading outside. In fact, for lack of protection against the elements the alterations in the painting and the texture of the stone are quite appreciable. However, for now, we should admire the lamps and the organs. We should also look up and contemplate the dome, a Gothic structure that was finished in 1445. At the angles it has the shields of Archbishop Lope de Mendoza, whose term ended in the same year the dome was completed. The balcony ringing the interior is from the 17th cen-

Triforium over Portico.

Detail, Keystone over Portico.

Central Aisle.

Cathedral Organ.*

St. John the Evangelist on
Portico of Glory.

tury. José de la Peña de Toro was responsible for the ornamentation. It measures 32 metres. The pulley system, made in 1602 in Vizcaya, was designed by Juan B. de Celma and is used to swing the "Botafumeiro", the enormous incense burner we will discuss later.

The first lamp we come upon as we walk towards the Portico comes from the Senate. Its donation to the cathedral was facilitated by the Compostelan Montero Ríos. We will also see the two **organs**, both from the 18th century, that are operated simultaneously from the same console. The organs' casings are the work of Manuel de la Viña, from 1704-1712. The lamp was exhibited at the International Exposition of Paris in 1855. Its decoration includes an abundance of acanthus leaves, branches, filaments and rock-crystal details. The donation was made to the cathedral by the family of the Prebendary Pedro Méndez Acuña.

General Information on the Portico

It is said that when King Ferdinand II visited Compostela in the 12th century, the western part of the cathedral was either unfinished or in poor condition, and the monarch decided to leave his palace architect, Mateo, in Santiago with a stipend so that he

Portico of Glory, General View.**

The Prophet Daniel.

Base of the Portico.

could carry out the work we are now admiring. Those were the days of the so-called "beati", codexes that copied the manuscript of San Beato de Liébana, who in the 8th century had recorded his observations on the Book of the Apocalyse. This served to popularise the final work on the Sacred Writing and the celebrated

Figure of Christ.

miniatures of the new architectural school headed by Magius. In fact, in the Portico there is a clear influence from the Book of the Apocalypse.

It was not a common practise to keep an architectural record of the work, and neither do we have an authorised description of the Portico. For this reason we can only hypothesize about the nature of the idea that was to be represented in this polychromed stone volume, destined, like the sculpture and painting in any church, to illustrate the mysteries of the faith to the faithful. The most probable hypothesis concerning the Portico contents that the work represents the Church in at least two of its most important dimensions: the military and the triumphant.

We known nothing about Master Mateo, though there are many conjectures that have been gleaned from data corresponding to what may, or may not, have been the man himself or relatives. Some say he was Galician; but others believe the influences in his art would indicate that he came from somewhere beyond the Pyrenees. What is not in doubt is his talent, marvelously reflected in this masterpiece. Is the statue that is seen kneeling and looking at the altar a self-portrait? Very possibly. If so, it reflects his piousness, his gratitude to God and his humility. It is known by the name "Santo dos Croques". "Croques" is a Galician word meaning — curiously — a blow to the head. In Compostela, it is a custom to tap one's head against the statue, so that the intelligence Mateo demonstrated might be transmitted to the modern-day visitor.

Christ, the Apostles and the Prophets

We can read in St. Paul's Letter to the Ephesians, which speaks of redemption, that "we are the fellow citizens of the saints and members of the family of God, built on the foundation of the Apostles and of the Prophets." We will see now how this doctrine was interpreted. The dominant figure of the Portico is Christ, nearly 3 metres in height, yet in a sitting position and showing the glorious wounds in his hands. Standing guard over him are the four evangelists, two on each side and easily identified by their corresponding symbols: Mark — the lion; Luke — the bull; John — the eagle; and Matthew, appearing without the child. In the lower part of the central arch, the angels

Portico of Glory, Partial View.*

Figure of St. James.*

The Apostles peter, Paul, St. James
and John the Evangelist.*

31

Musicians on the upper part of central arch (left) and human figures on left arch (right).

Trumpeting Angel.

bear instruments associated with the Passion. On the upper part, twenty-four musicians, the Elders of the Apocalypse, bear musical instruments, too, among which is a "organistrum", with strings and a geared cog for plucking them. The small images that are beneath these — miniatures being used to evoke the multitude — represent the believers who have already made it to heaven.

The figures on the right are the Apostles; beginning in the middle, we see Peter, Paul, James and his brother, John the Evangelist. Those on the left are the Prophets; in the same order as the Apostles are Moses, Isaiah, Daniel and Jeremiah. The monstrous figures on the bases remind one of the hybrid guardians of the oriental palaces in Assyria and Babilonia. They may represent the vices, being subdued by the Church. The face of the man that is opening the mouths of two lions with his hands, in the centre, may represent the Celestial Father, the Creator of the Universe.

Jews and Gentiles

The Bible divides humanity into two groups: Jews, the members of the tribes of Israel, a group to which Christ belonged, and Gentiles. Here we also have the two divisions of humanity called to form part of the Church. On the right, between the central and lateral arches, are nude figures, one of which is being covered with a cloak by an angel, a symbol of baptism and grace. On the left, are the Jews, also nude, but bearing a tablet that brings to mind the books of the Old Testament, the Jewish Scriptures.

The arch on the right shows strange animals clawing a man. Without a doubt they represent the enslaving vices. On the left arch we can make out three archivolts adorned with foliage and some human figures. The people represent humanity awaiting the coming of the Mesiah. On the lower archivolt, Adam and Eve see amongst them the figure of God's Messenger, who has come to free the universe of the sin they introduced.

Detail, the Christological Column.

Capital showing the Holy Trinity.

The Christological Column

In the middle of the central arch, beneath the figure of the seated St. James the Greater, who holds a tau-shaped staff and a tablet bearing the inscription "the Lord sent me", we have a column of white porphyry that offers us a lesson in Christology. Here, artistic representations bring together human origin and the divine origin of Christ. The human figure appears on the co- lumn shaft; from the chest of an elderly figure lying on the ground — perhaps Isaiah or Jesse, David's father — a tree sprouts. Entangled in the tree limbs are various figures, of which two can be clearly identified: David, holding a musical instru- ment, and Solomon, holding the royal sceptre. Above the ca- nopy of the tree floats the figure of Mary. The fact that she is not touching the tree could be a suggestion of the faith at the church in Compostela in the 12th century, since the mystery of the Immaculate Conception would not be defined as Church dogma until the 19th century.

Figure of David.

The capital represents the Holy Trinity, that is, the divinity of Christ. The figuration is a common one: the Father is a crowned

Figure of Solomon.

elder, and upon his knee sits his Son. The Holy Spirit is symbolized by a dove, a way of reminding us of the evangelical passage of the baptism of Christ, in which it is written that "once Jesus was baptised, he emerged from the water and the skies opened and he saw the Holy Spirit descend in the form of a dove and alight upon him." The dove and fire are images with which the Sacred Scriptures refer to the Holy Spirit, doubtlessly in order to emphasise the fire of love that the Holy Spirit produces in man's heart and the purity of life provided by the Holy Spirit's gifts.

"Santo dos Croques"

This Galician expression is traditionally used to refer to the kneeling figure looking up towards the altar from behind the Portico. It is believed to be the self-portrait of Master Mateo. It is said that the director of the Portico project reproduced his likeness for an earlier figure and that the Archbishop recriminated him for the prentious act of including himself among the representatives of the Triumphant Church when he was still a member of the Militant Church. It was then perhaps that the Master decided to render himself in this humble and grateful manner. As curious as it may sound, "croque" means "a hit, eit-

Handprint, "Santo Dos Croques".

Worshippers Before "Santo Dos Croques".

her given or received by the head" in the Galician language. Pilgrims tend to touch their heads to the statue in an attempt to receive from Mateo his unique inspiration. According to others, "croque" has its origin in the Oc language, also known as Provençal or Limousin, and means "curl". Thus, the traditional name for the statue would be something like, "the Curly-haired Saint".

Apart from the folkloric headbutt of Master Mateo, it should be pointed out that pilgrims also traditionally place their hands in the space between the tree branches in the central column. While some speak of receiving as many graces as the fingers on one's hand, in reality there is no evidence to justify this explanation.

V CAPILLAS DE LA GIROLA

Towards the Apse Choir

Now we'll follow the right aisle towards the head of the cathedral. We pass by a door on our right to the Chapel of the Relics and the Chapel of St. Ferdinand, the latter now the Treasury, which we'll visit later. If we turn into the right transverse cross-section, the first door is that of the **Sacristy**, which is not open to the public. It is part of the work carried out in the 16th century for storing relics. It contains 25 pictures in copper, twelve Flemish ones from the 18th century in the lower part that represent the 12 articles of the Creed, each of which is attributed to one of the Apostles. The other 13 represent scenes from the life of the Virgin Mary and Jesus. There are also paintings by Gregorio Ferro, Juan Antonio Bouzas and Modesto Brocos. The next door leads to the cloister and the museums. Next to this door is the **Clavijo Tympanum**, with young maidens thanking St. James for having pardoned their contribution. The sculpture comes from the cloister, which was built on the orders of Archbishop Gelmírez. On the opposite corner, there is a place for holy water that is believed to have come from the 9th-century church. It is said that Almanzor watered his horse there.

Sacristy Door.

Clavijo Tympanum, General View.**

The **Chapel of Pilar** was built with the contributions made by Archbishop Fray Antonio de Monroy in the 17th century. The mausoleum that holds his remains is crowed by a statue of a praying figure and was done by Fernández de Sande. In the construction of this chapel, the contributions of the two Baroque masters, Andrade and Casas, complement one another. The dome is octogonal. The altarpiece, in marble, was sketched by Casas and built by Romay. The stone figure of the Virgin Pilar was brought from Zaragoza. The other figures weresculpted by Sande, who found fosilised shells to adorn the Apostle's shoulder cape

The following chapel has two names: **Piedad** (Pietá), in honor of the Virgin, and **Mondragón**, for its founder, the Prebendary Juan Ibáñez de Mondragón, who lived in the 16th century. The style is Flourid Ogival. The representation of the Pietá, or the Descent of Christ from the Cross, is done in baked clay which some claim is actually lava from Mt. Vesuvius. The next chapel, that of **St. Peter**, **Azucena** and the **Magistrate**, the latter referring to

Chapel of Our Lady of the Pillar.

Mondragón Chapel.

the patron of the founder, Mencía de Andrade, who had the chapel built in 1571. The altarpiece, Baroque in style, was desinged by Fernando de Casas and built by Francisco das Moas. The figure of St. Jude is widely venerated for helping the faithful solve particularly difficult problems.

Detail, Columns of Door of the Saint.

The Holy Door and The Chapel of the Saviour

The **Holy Door**, which is only opened in Holy Years (when 25 July, the feastday of the martyr St. James the Greater falls on Sunday, a phenomenon occurring in intervals of 11, 6, 5 and 6 years), is one of the cathedral's seven minor doors mentioned in the Calixtine Codex, the first guidebook for the Route of St. James, which Pope Calixtus had written in the 12th century. On the tablets seen on both sides of the door, one can read, in Latin, an inscription saying, "All Peoples Will Come and They Will Say: Glory to You, Lord."

The **Chapel of the Saviour** was the first chapel to be built. In fact, the work on the current cathedral in 1075 actually began here. The two capitals on the entrance bear two inscriptions in-

Retable of the Chapel of the Saviour.

dicating that the work started under the aegis of Bishop Diego Peláez and King Alphonse VI. The same message was also etched into the walls; however, the opening up of the vaulted niches has made a good part of it disappear. Here, Archbishop Alonso de Fonseca certified the "Compostela", the accreditation awarded to pilgrims for having made the holy trek (and still awarded today). The confessors in different languages, known as "lenguajeros", were also stationed here and would give Holy Communion to all those with the proper documentation.

The altar, in polychromed stone, was designed by Juan de Alava and was paid for by Archbishop Alonso III de Fonseca in the 16th century. Two Compostelan bishop-saints — Pedro de Mezonzo, attributed to la Salve, and Rosendo. The Fonseca family shield, bearing 5 stars, reminds us of the munificence of one of the family members in the ornamentation in the chapel, which has been preserved exactly as it was designed in the Romanesque Period.

This chapel is also known as the **French Chapel** after St. Louis of the French because King Charles V, the Learned, of Fran-

General view of the Chapel of the Saviour.

ce set up a foundation for celebrating the holy mass here in 1380. This foundation would later back Louis XI in the next century.

At our backs is the chapel directly behind the main altar, which served as the sacristy as well as a confessional, a place for Communion and the place where the "Compostela" certificate was accredited until Alphonse III moved these functions to the Chapel of the Saviour. Then it was called the **Chapel of Confession** and also the Chapel of Mary Magdalen, in honour of the Bible's most model penitent. Also in honor of Mary Magdalen is a figure on the altar in the Chapel of the Saviour. Pedro de Valle, in 1671, did the altarpiece, in which three scenes from the life of St. James the Greater are shown: martyrdom, the transference of his remains and his burial. Between the altar itself and the altarpiece is a star crowning the Apostle's mausoleum. In front of the altar is the place where Archbishop Juan de Sanclemente had the Apostle's remains hidden, in 1589, to protect them from Drake.

From La Blanca Chapel to the Chapel of the Holy Spirit

The following chapel is dedicated to the Virgin Mary and is known as the **Chapel of Our Lady in White**. It is also known as the **Chapel of the Españas**, because one of the family names of the patrons buried here is **España**, along with Torrado and Arousa. The entrance arch is from the 16th century, while the consecrated cross is from the year 1211. The ceiling has a groin vault with irregularly shaped ribbing. The Neo-Gothic altar was done by Magarños in the 20th century. The figure of the Immaculate Virgin is by Gregorio Fernández, from 1747. The other two images of the Virgin, from the second half of the 20th century, are the English Virgin of Walsingham and the Catalan Virgin of Montserrat. This chapel was also where the Brotherhood of San Eloy, the patron saint of silverworkers, was started.

Jácome García rebuilt the chapel of **St. John the Apostle** and **St. Susan**, the co-patron saint of the city of Santiago de Compostela, in the 16th century. The figures on the Baroque altarpiece — St. John, from the 15th century, and St. Susan, by Mariñas in 1902 — give the chapel its name. For several centuries, the parish church of St. John the Apostle was actually this

Chapel of Our Lady in White.

Chapel of St. Bartholomew.

Sepulchre of Prebendary Diego de Castilla in the Chapel of St. Bartholomew.

chapel. Frenchilla did the figure of Santo Domingo de la Calzada, donated by the Ministry for Public Works in the Saint's Year of 1965.

The name of the Chapel of Santa Fe de Conques is now known by two other names: **The Chapel of the Virgin of Good Council and of St. Bartholomew**. The Virgin is the main figure,but the foundation named in honour of St. Bartholomew and organised by the Prebendary Gómez Rodríguez de Sotomayor in 1516 managed to have the saint's name added on. The storied capitals are worthy of note, too. The Plateresque series of stories is the work of the Flemish engraver, Mateo Arnao, who also did the sepulchre, in Coimbra marble, of the Prebendary Diego de Castilla, the great-grandson of King Pedro, the Cruel, who died in 1521. The **Chapel of the Conception** has two entrances. The earliest one is on the left and it used to provide access to the Chapel of Santa Cruz. The Brotherhood of the Clerics of Prima — another name being the **Chapel of Prima** —

Figure of the Virgin, Chapel of
the Conception.

View of Chapel of the Conception.

Altarpiece, Chapel of the
Holy Spirit.

Chapel of the Holy Spirit.

was granted permission in 1525 to enlarge its area in the cathedral and to dedicate an altar to the Conception. That was when the archway on the right was opened. The stone figure of the Virgin was done by Cornelis of Holland in the 16th century. It was repainted and bedecked in jewels in the 18th century. A novelty in the iconography of the Virgin is existence of the Child in her arms holding a cross. In 1721, Diego Fernández de Sande sculpted the Descent, while Antonio Alfonsín and Manuel de Leis did the others. On the floor is the practically unrecognisable sepulchre of the Baroque artist Domingo Antonio de Andrade.

The site of one of the old doors, the door of St. Mary, has been occupied since the 13th century by the **Chapel of the Holy Spirit**, reserved for Chaplains of Sancti Spiritus, later called the Prebendaries of Sancti Spiritus. The chapel was enlarged in the 14th century and rebuilt in the 16th and 17th centuries. The altar and the image of the Virgin of Solitude come from the retrochoir and were placed here in 1945. The Virgin figure was done in Madrid in 1666. Archbishop Fray Rafael de Vélez donated the shoulder cape in the 19th century. In the 18th century, Antonio Morales did the altar and the seating in silver. The altar platform, the angels and the ornaments are the work of Francisco Rodríguez. The Way of the Cross is from the 15th century.

Detail, Sepulchre of Archbishop
Alonso Moscoso.

Sepulchre of Juan de Melgarejo.

Fresco of the Descent.

Our Lady of Solitude, Chapel of the Holy Spirit.

A Parish for Foreigners and Basques

Going up the stairs now, we come to the parish church of **Corticela**. The building has an earlier oratory where Benedictine monks used to come to pray to the Apostle. The current structure is the fruit of work that continued from the 11th century until the beginning of the 13th century. It was restored in the later half of the 20th century. It was set up in the Middle Ages as a place of worship for foreigners and Basques. The doorway, Romanesque in style, contains an Adoration of the Magi motif, frequently found in Compostela because of that fact that the Magi were also pilgrims as well as representatives of different peoples, which brings out the universal nature of the St. James pilgrimage. The Virgin of Solace is the predominant figure. The Baby Jesus of Prague was the patron of the Tecelanes. The artisans who worked in the mine-

Corticela Church.

ral jet also had a figure of St. Stephen, their protector, here. The Oration of Jesus in the Orchard and the Virgin of the Miraculous Medal are objects of wide veneration, despite the fact that their iconography does not correspond to the architectonic purity of the church, at first to connected the cathedral.

As we go back down, on our right is a chapel dedicated to **St. Andrew**, once the main site of the parish of the same name and previously situated in the area currently occupied by the Chapel of Our Lady of the Pillar. A lateral altar is dedicated to the Virgin of Mt. Carmel; the other to St. Joseph. In a niche is an image of the Virgin of Luján, a gift of the Doello-Teruelo family, which has replaced the one brought by Eva Perón. The chapel was built in the 17th century.

Chapel of St. Anthony.

VI CHAPELS OF THE LEFT NAVE

From the Chapel of St. Anthony to the Chapel of Christo of Burgos

The **Chapel of St. Anthony**, currently associated with St. Nicholas (whose chapel was destroyed so as to open passage to the Corticela Church), was also the main site of a parish, that dedicated to St. Fructuoso, now in the old Church of the Angustias de Abajo. The altarpiece is from the 18th century. The figure of the Virgin of Fatima was brought here from the site of the Portuguese miracle in 1948.

We leave the Azabachería entranceway now and find ourselves before the **Chapel of St. Catherine**, dedicated to the saint of Alexandria. The chapel dates from before the 16th century. A

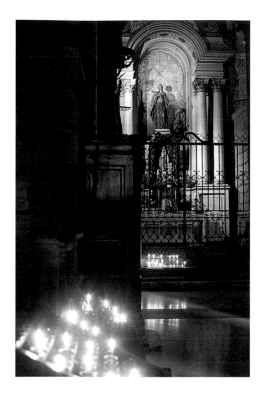

reproduction of the apparition of the Virgin Mary at Lourdes can be seen.

Chapel of St. Catherine.

The sculptor Gambino did the figure of **St. James the Knight** in the second half of the 18th century. This rendition of St. James is an attempt to show the Apostle's protection of Spain through the centuries and is based on the legend of St. James' appearing to King Ramiro I at the Battle of Clavijo (actually involving Ordoño I, not Ramiro). This scene occupies the door that once gave access to the following chapel, **Lope de Mendoza**, which is also called the **Chapel of Communion** and the **Chapel of the Sacred Heart**. Lope de Mendoza, the Archbishop of Santiago de Compostela from 1399 to 1445, was its patron. The alabaster image of the Virgin of Pardon on the right near the entrance, shows the Archbishop on his knees, pleading for the Lord's clemency following Mary's intercession on his behalf. The current chapel, Neo-classical in style and domed, was done by Archbishop Rajoy in the 18th century. He had Ferro Caaveiro design it and the work was done

Chapel of the Communion.

Chapel of the Christ of Burgos

by Del Río and Nogueira. The altarpiece is by Lens and comes from the Chapel of the Relics. The statues of the four Church doctors in the niches are the work of Gregorio Español and Juan Vila. From the 16th to the 18th century, university classes were given here. The Archbishops Mendoza and Rajoy are both buried here.

The Archbishop Pedro Carrillo y Acuña had the **Chapel of Christ of Burgos**, also known as the **Carrillo Chapel**, built. It was built in the form of a Greek cross, with a dome, by Mechor de Velasco y Agüero beginning in 1665. The beautiful figure of Christ is a copy of the one in Burgos and was sculpted in that city in 1754. Melchor de Prado made the Baroque lateral altars, where we can see two evangelical scenes: The intercession of St. Salome on behalf of her children, on the right, and St. Peter Weeping After Denying Christ, on the left. The side sepulchres are those of Archbishop Carrillo and García Cuesta. The one on the floor is that of Archbishop Zacarías Martínez Núñez.

MUSEUMS

Now that we have finished viewing the cathedral's interior, we shall visit the museums, which are located in three areas of the cathedral, two inside and one outside, which we'll visit last.

I CHAPEL OF THE RELICS AND TREASURY

Once finished with the visit to the Chapel of the Christ of Burgos, also known as Carrillo Chapel, one should cross the three aisles and enter the door directly ahead. This leads to the Chapel of the Relics and the Chapel of St. Ferdinand, currently in use as a showroom for the cathedral's most valuable works of art.

The **Chapel of the Relics** is usually only open to the public for about half-an-hour each morning, during the holding of mass (9:30 weekdays). It was built between 1521 and 1529 and is attributed to Juan de Alava. In 1921 a fire destroyed the altarpiece by Fernando Cabrera and all the figures done by Gregorio Español. In 1925 Maximino Magariños fashioned a new altarpiece out of cedar from a design by Rafael de la Torre. One can see

St. James the Pilgrim.

Bust of St. James the Greater.

a good deal of the chapel through the glass door.

The relics number 140 and include urns, busts, small monstrances and a variety of figures. Of special note are the head of St. James the Lesser, enclosed in a silver bust with an enamel face. It was donated by Archbishop Berenguel de Landoira in the 14th century, while the collar was given by Suero de Quiñones in the 15th century. There is also a figure dating from the 13th and 14th centuries of St. James the Greater, with a bone relic, donated by the Parisian Godofredo Coquatriz. Lastly, there is a figure of St. Theresa of Jesus, with a tooth as a relic and the signature of the saint from Avila. This piece is from the 19th century.

But there are many other objects on display in this chapel: A facsimile of the cross, donated by Alphonse III in 874; the crystal and gold Italian pax, donated by King Charles II in 1638; cornucopias with biblical motifs, done in silver and adorned with stones; the alabaster series of scenes that was donated by the English priest Gudgar in 1456; a chalice and paten said to belong to San Rosendo and a figure of St. James the Pilgrim, in gilted silver, sent from Paris in the 15th century.

From outside, one cannot see the royal sepulchres, moved here from the Chapel of St. Catherine in 1535. On the right is

St. Theresa.

Niche, Chapel of St. Ferdinand.

that of King Ferdinand II of Leon, whose prone likeness is possible the work of Master Mateo, and those of King Alphonse IX and Count Traba, Pedro Froilaz; on the left is that of the wife of Alphonse VII, Berenguela, and those of Count Ramón of Burgundy, Alphonse VII's father, and Juana de Castro, the wife of Peter I of Castile.

In the vestibule are paintings by Cancela from the last century. There is another attributed to Murillo which shows shows the apparition of the Virgin to San Félix de Catalicio. There is also a sepulchre stone dedicated to Bishop Teodomiro of Iria Flavia, who died in 847 and during whose term the remains of St. James were rediscovered. It was precisely due to the rediscovery that Bishop Teodomiro decided to be born here and not within his bishopric.

The **Chapel of St. Ferdinand** was, for nearly a century, the Relic Showroom of the cathedral, in the 16th and 17th centuries. It is named after St. Ferdinand III, the king who called himself "the standard bearer of St. James". He accompanied his father, Alphonse IX, to the consecration ceremony of the cathedral in the year 1211, and, as king in 1232, returned as a pilgrim. The figure representing him on the altar was sculpted by Seoane in the year 1676. The two frescoes representing the Ascension of Christ and the Assumption of the Virgin Mary date from 1540.

Upon entering, we see the **tabernacle**, done in gilded silver by Antonio de Arfe in the 16th century. At its foot are six figures in relief representing scenes from St. James' life, beginning with his vocation as an apostle and ending with the transporting of his remains. Also included are the miracle of the hanging and the reborn cock as told in the Calixtine Codex. In 24 smaller reliefs there are scenes of the life of Christ. Four Church doctors pay tribute to the Eucharist. There is a **St. Christopher** in coral on a silver and bronze background, of Italian origin and said to have been donated by John of Austria. another figure is that of St. James, done in jet by E. Mayer in 1919. The **silver cup** that is used for the National Offering ceremony was donated by the Dukes of Montpensier, the Duchess being the sister of Queen Elizabeth II. The **hammer** is used to open the Holy Door. We can also see trays in the shape of shells, a figure linked to the Jacobean tradition, and various **chalices**, **paxes** and **other liturgical objects**. A pair of **candalabras** and a **crucifix** made of rock crystal with gold settings, a golden statue of Jesus and a **dis-**

play case containing the biretta of Cardinal Quiroga Palacios, who died in 1971, complement the tryptych that was donated by the province of Orense. The **tabernacle** was made of jewels belonging to the Ferreiro de la Maza family. Like the tryptych, it comes from the workshop of Angel Iglesias inOrense. Among the **ornaments**, there are 16th-century pluvials and chausables and dalmatics from the 18th century.

Sepulchre of St. Ferdinand II of Leon.

Bust of St. Pauline.

Cloister Door.

II CLOISTER

If we turn right into the smaller transverse nave, we can enter the **cloister** and the **museums** by way of the second door. The current cloister is the cathedral's third in its history. The first two were built during Archbishop Gelmírez's lifetime. The first one was possibly the work of Master Mateo in the 12th century, while the second one was built in the 13th century. The one we see now was constructed between 1521 and 1590 and among those who worked on it were Juan de Alava, Jácome García, Rodrigo Gil de hontañón, Juan de Herrera and Gaspar de Arce. It was built on the initiative of Archbishop Alphonse III de Fonseca, and we can see his shield at the end of the entrance hall.

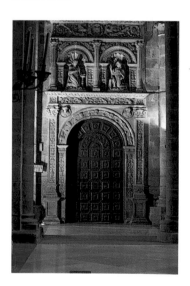

General View of
Cloister. **

On the right, as we go towards the museum, is the **Chapel of Dawn**, established in 1529 by the Prebendary Gómez Vallo for the celebration of holy mass each day at dawn. The 18th-century altarpiece, which replaced an earlier one, is by Cornelis of Hollanda and shows scenes of the transfiguration of the Lord.

At the end of the wall closing off this part of the cloister is the **Capitular Archive**, where important documents pertaining to the cathedral, and Galicia in general, are kept. Some, such as those referring to the Vow of St. James, have even greater geographical importance. Among these documents is the Calixtine Codex, cathedral registers A, B, C and D with documentation from the 9th to the 14th century, original diplomas, etc. The Archive is open to researchers.

View of Archive.

Miniature belonging to Register A.

IV LIBRARY AND CAPITULAR HALL

"Botafumeiro".

In the same area of the cloister are two rooms. The first is the **Capitular Library**, the contents of which were procurred by the Prebendaries Pedro de Acuña Malvar and Diego Juan de Ulloa. It was built in the 18th century by Ferro Caaveiro and Arias Varela. There is a movable pulpit, and frescoes adorn the walls.

To the left are two **Botafumeiros**. The first was a gift from the Brotherhood of Provisional Standard-bearers in 1971. The second one is older, having been made in 1851. The botafumeiro is a giant incense burner used during solemn processions. It was also used to create religious ambience in the cathedral itself when pilgrims were still sleeping there, up until the 18th century

The **Capitular Hall**, the next room, is so named because it was where the various prebendary organisations that constituted the cathedral's Governing Chapter would meet. In Latin, the word "Capitulum" means "meeting of prebendary monks." While there may be influences from Casas and Nóvoa in the architectural rendering of the hall, the project was the work of Lucas Ferro Caaveiro. The vault, in granite, was stuccoed and gilded by Aguiar. The altar's frontispiece is by Bartolomé Sernini, who also worked on the Royal Palace in Madrid. The figure of St. James the Pilgrim is

View of Library Hall.

by Gambino. The canopy, from the Royal Tapistry Factory of Madrid, was designed by Guillermo de Anglois for Charles III's room. The other tapistries, some of which are Flemish and others also from the Madrid Royal Factory, are based on designs by Teniers and show scenes of the lives of Achilles and Scippio. The brazier is from the 18th century and has Jacobean motifs. The two boxes are made of holy wood, boulle, mother-of-pearl and marble. The picture of the Virgin of Guadalupe was donated by the Archbishop Antonio de Monroy, who was born in Mexico.

V TAPESTRY MUSEUM

On the right is a **clock** made by a Dominican priest. It bears an inscription in Latin that means, "Time measures everything; but I, made by the hand of God, measure time." Two tapistries, one on the right and the other on the left, are by Ginés de Aguirre; the one before us is by Teniers. The image of St. Salome is from the 18th century

The **First Hall**, on our right, has tapistries made from the sketches by an anonymous artist and also by Ginés de Aguirre, Teniers and José del Castillo, who represented the Sacred Family asking

Interior of Cathedral
Library.*

Cathedral Chapter
Hall.*

Tapestry from Santa
Barbara Royal Factory,
from a Goya cartoon.

some hunters for alms. These were all made at the Santa Barbara
Royal Factory. There are two examples of cordovan. The banner of
the flagship in the Battle of lepanto, measuring 17.5 metres, was
donated by John of Austria in 1571.

The **Second Hall**: the story of Achilles and other mythological
themes relating to love were taken from sketches by Rubens and
his disciple Van Thulden. They were made at Flemish workshops in
Brussels by Jan Raez and Erasmus Oorlofs. The ark, used for storing
valuables, dates from 1742.

The **Third Hall**: the tapistries in this hall, showing folkloric, ru-
ral scenes, were made at the Santa Barbara Royal Factory from
sketches by Teniers. Two are of special note: the bowlers, which
appears to have made at the workshop of Jean Metrer in Lille, and
that of the pauper asking for alms, which may have been done by
Antonio González Ruíz.

The **Fourth Hall**: two of these tapistries are by Tenier, the one
in blue tones showing the butchering of a pig. The others are Goya's brother-in-law, Francisco Bayeu y Subías. The one showing an
elderly man playing a Zamoran bagpipe appears to have been the
work of González Ruíz.

The **Fifth Hall**: all of the tapistries in this hall are from sketches by Goya and were donated by Pedro de Acuña, Charles IV's
Minister. They were made at the Santa Barbara Royal Factory. The
oils on wood are by Gregorio Ferro (1805-1810).

Tapestries showing scenes from the life of Achilles, from cartoons of Rubens.

VI   ARCHEOLOGICAL MUSEUM

After visiting the Tapistry Museum, one might wish to move on to the Archaeological Museum. In the first of the two halls there are Jacobean scenes in wood and alabaster, an anonymous work from 15th-century England; there is also a tympanum showing Jesus entering Jerusalem, also anonymous, from the 14th century. The figure of a seated St. James dates from the 13th century. A tympanum of the Adoration is from the 14th century. The Virgin of O and the Archangel Gabriel is from the 15th century. The cruxification, from Celma, is from the 16th century. And there are also pieces done in wood by Gregorio Español and his students, Joseph's Dream by Dávila, Mateo de Prado and Master Fadrique. In the last area are books, documents and maps, including some by Obradoiro and Casas y Nóvoa. The Clock Tower is by Andrade.

At the entrance to the **Lower Hall**, there is a cast of St. James among cypress trees, based on a piece by Master Esteban from the

Tympanum of the Adoration, 14th century.

Body of St. James in Queen Lupa's ox cart. Polychromed wood, Archaeological Museum.

Platerías façade (circa 1100). Also of note is the rosette window from the exterior façade of the Portico of Glory, replaced by the current Baroque one. The rosette was made in Mateo's workshop; also from his workshop are several pieces of the choir's woodworking. And finally, there are diverse materials from the excavations carried out underneath the cathedralstarting in 1946. There is another hall on the right as we leave the lower hall, in which we

find parts of an ancient road, a graphic reconstitution and various pieces from the Choir by Master Mateo and of Caligula's milliary, from the year 40 AD.

VII   CRYPT BENEATH THE PORTICO

By going down the Obradoiro stairway, we come to what is commonly called the Old Cathedral, which is actually a crypt built to link the different levels. It is part of the work done by Mateo and has three plans: the Portico belongs to the central plan. There are various fagments of the western façade attributed to the Master of the Wet Cloths, a contemporary of Master Mateo. Some of the pieces may come from the crypt's doorway. We should also mention the stand of columns, which bears the weight of the work above it.

THE FIRST PRINTING OF THIS BOOK, PUBLISHED BY ALDEASA, WAS FINISHED
ON THE 31ST OR MARCH, 1993 IN THE GRAPHIC STUDIOS OF
HERACLIO FOURNIER, LTD. VITORIA.